Iris Wall, CRACKER COWGIRL

By Carol Matthews Rey

Illustrated by Eldon Lux

PELICAN PUBLISHING COMPANY
Gretna 2012

Carol and Eldon wish to express their gratitude to Miss Iris for sharing her story and allowing us to tell it! We've had a great ride! We'll see you again down the road!

To JRR, who I love more than I love myself, and to all of our own cowgirls and cowboys—CMR

Thanks to Miss Iris, for her inspiration; Carol, for being such a delightful partner in this venture; and to my best friend, my wife Lynn, who is a genuine Florida Cracker Cowgirl also—EL

Copyright © 2012
By Carol Matthews Rey

Illustrations copyright © 2012
By Eldon Lux

Library of Congress Cataloging-in-Publication Data

Rey, Carol Matthews
  Iris Wall, cracker cowgirl / by Carol Matthews Rey ; illustrated by Eldon Lux.
     p. cm.
  ISBN 978-1-4556-1525-4 (hardcover : alk. paper)—ISBN 978-1-4556-1526-1 (e-book) 1. Wall, Iris Pollock, 1929—Juvenile literature. 2. Women ranchers—Florida—Biography—Juvenile literature. 3. Ranchers—Florida—Biography—Juvenile literature. 4. Cowgirls—Florida—Biography—Juvenile literature. 5. Ranching—Florida—History—Juvenile literature. 6. Ranch life—Florida—Juvenile literature. 7. Florida--Biography—Juvenile literature. I. Lux, Eldon, ill. II. Title.
  SF194.2.W35R49 2012
  636'.01092—dc23
  [B]
                          2011036815

Printed in Singapore
Published by Pelican Publishing Company, Inc.
1000 Burmaster Street, Gretna, Louisiana 70053

It was 1929, the year of the Great Depression,
before electric lights, running water, or telephones
came to the woods of South Florida, that a girl named
Iris was born—a girl who loved to ride horses and
hunt cows—a Cracker cowgirl.

Iris and her two younger sisters and brother grew up surrounded by a family of Cracker cowhunters. Nobody really knew for sure where the term "cracker" came from, maybe from the Florida cowboys who cracked cow whips to move cattle.

Iris's grandpa was an expert at making cow whips. In the evening when everyone gathered on the porch to visit, the men practiced popping their whips. Sometimes the kids held matchsticks in their hands, arms straight out, and quicker than hot grease poppin' on a griddle, the men would knock those matchsticks right out! "Tha-waack!" Usually, the only kid brave enough to hold one was Iris.

When Iris's grandma needed something, all she had to do was go outside and pop the cow whip a couple of times, "Ka-thwaack" "Ka-thwaack," and all her grandkids came running.

In those days, Iris's family had no television or even a radio for entertainment. But, on Friday nights, no matter where they lived, all of Iris's aunts, uncles, and cousins came home to Indiantown for the weekend and brought their harps, fiddles, guitars, and banjos. When it got dark they built a bonfire in the front yard and played and sang till midnight.

Iris's mother loved to sing. She remembered the words to every song she ever heard, and she taught all the kids to sing:
"Fly's in the buttermilk,
    Shoo, fly, shoo,
Fly's in the buttermilk,
    Shoo, fly, shoo,
Fly's in the buttermilk,
    Shoo, fly, shoo,
Skip to my Lou my darlin'!"

While other girls were learning to sew, quilt, embroider, or crochet, Iris was busy learning to cowhunt with her daddy. She had her own horse, Dollie, a little, blue roan Cracker mare. They were best friends. Iris rode Dollie everywhere—fishing, swimming, hunting, and visiting the neighbors.

But the thing that Iris loved best in the whole world was cowhunting. She'd wake up before dawn, saddle Dollie, whistle for the dogs, and off they'd go.

At roundup time Iris and Daddy would camp out for a week at a time. They carried their food in their saddle pockets: strips of white bacon, some cold biscuits, and sweet potatoes.

When it was time to eat, Iris gathered wood for a fire. Daddy rode out into a pond and dipped up some water in a quart-sized peach can tied with baling wire. That was his coffee pot. Then he'd cut and trim some palmetto fans for sticks, put the meat on one end, and plant the other end in the ground by the fire.

Once, while they were working cows, a great big yearling broke out of the pens and came straight at them! Daddy jumped on Dollie and roped the yearling. When the cow hit the end of the rope, it jerked the saddle to Dollie's side and Daddy fell off!

What a sight it was to watch Dollie. Saddle hanging from her side, stirrups flapping, Dollie herded that mad yearling away from Daddy.

Iris and her daddy hunted cows in the scrub like Easter eggs. They penned and branded calves, cleared and burned pasture, and doctored sick cows all day long.

Iris's daddy liked to trade horses. He'd bring home a truck load of young, green horses from Tampa and say, "Go to 'em, gal!" That's exactly what Iris did. In no time, she'd have those wild horses tame and sweet enough for a baby to ride. No horse ever got the best of her.

Mules were a different matter. Once, Daddy brought home a mule named Isaac. It seemed like Isaac's purpose in life was to see how many times he could throw Iris off.

He bucked!
He kicked!
He twitched!
He twirled!

He threw her off so many times that
Iris lost count! They tried to sell Isaac
once or twice, but he always came back.

When Iris was in high school, the Circle T Rodeo came to town. To announce the start of the rodeo, Iris rode out into the arena carrying the United States flag.

Early rodeos had no events for women. Iris rode the bulls anyway.

"Heeeeeeeere comes a twistin', turnin', buckin' bundle of blue twisted steel! How long can she hold on?" cried the announcer.

In 1948 Iris married her childhood friend and high school sweetheart, Homer "Cowboy" Wall. When they were in the eighth grade, Iris and Homer had parts in the school play, *Aunt Drusilla's Garden*. Iris was Aunt Drusilla and Homer was the gardener. Iris loved the gardener for the rest of his life.

Iris and Homer began their life together camping in the Everglades, hunting cows, and cutting fence posts. They worked for five years cutting posts to fence other people's ranches. Finally they saved enough money to buy their own land, High Horse Ranch, in Indiantown.

Before long, they had a family: three little Cracker cowgirls who all loved to go cowhunting. The girls hunted cows in the scrub like Easter eggs. They penned and branded calves, cleared and burned pasture, and doctored sick cows with their mother and daddy, all day long.

Iris and Homer lived a long and happy life together. Someone once asked Homer what their secret was. His reply was simple.

"Iris loves me more than she loves herself and I love her more than I love myself."

Homer died in 1994.

Iris is still cowhunting.

Miss Iris has hunted cows for almost eighty years. She still keeps a herd of Cracker cattle on her ranch and she still rides a Cracker horse. She is often seen riding around her ranch, in a wagon filled with school children, looking for wildlife and telling stories about what it was like growing up in old Florida.

And Miss Iris still loves to sing. She remembers the words to every song she ever heard, and she teaches all the kids in the wagon to sing:

"Cow's in the cornfield.
 What'll I do?
Cow's in the cornfield,
 What'll I do?
Cow's in the cornfield,
 What'll I do?
Skip to my Lou my darlin'!"

Glossary

Cow whip—a long, braided, leather whip, used by Florida cowboys for five hundred years. The cowboys used the sound of the cracking whip to steer the cattle out of the scrub and in the direction they wanted. The cracking sound is as loud as a rifle shot and can be heard for several miles.

Cracker cattle—small to medium-sized animals descended from the original cattle brought to Florida by Ponce de Leon in the 1500s. Some were left behind and formed wild herds that were used by the Indians and became the starter stock for early settlers all over the South. Florida is America's oldest cattle-raising state.

Cracker horses—small horses known for their strength and stamina. They are descendants of Spanish horses brought to Florida in the 1500s by Ponce de Leon. They adapted to Florida's environment and were perfectly suited for hunting cows. The Cracker horse is the official Heritage Horse for the State of Florida.

Cracker house—South Florida pioneers constructed simple "cracker box" houses made out of pine. The houses were built on brick pilings to protect the house from flooding and to keep them cool. The extra space under the house gave the people a large storage area and a place for their animals to sleep. They usually had a porch on two or three sides that served as a sitting room.

Cow dogs—one of the few working breeds that originates in the United States. Florida cowhunters needed the help of their dogs to chase stray cattle out of the hammocks, scrubs, and swamps.

White bacon—or "fatback" came from the meat of wild hogs. The meat was salted to preserve it. Early pioneers had a "hogmark" that they registered with the state. Any time they came upon a sow and pigs, they marked the pigs to claim them.

Florida cowhunter or Cracker cowhunter—words used to describe Florida cowboys. In pioneer days, people hunted wild cattle to form their herds. Florida cowboys called themselves cowhunters.

Florida Cracker—a term used by some Floridians to indicate that their family has lived in Florida for many generations. It is a source of pride to be descended from "frontier people," a hardy, enduring group, who could live without modern conveniences.

Great Depression—a period of hard economic times in the United States

Indiantown—a town in South Florida named after the Seminole Indians who lived there before the early pioneers. Betty Mae Jumper, the first woman to be named Seminole Tribal Council Leader, was born in Indiantown. In 1927, railroad developer S. Davies Warfield built the Seminole Inn, a train station, and Warfield Elementary School in Indiantown. King Edward VIII of England gave up his throne to marry Mr. Warfield's niece, Wallis.

Scrub—wild shrubs and grasslands

Yearling—a horse between one and two years old

More about Iris Wall

In 2006 Iris Pollock Wall was presented the Woman of the Year in Agriculture Award by Florida Agriculture Commissioner Charles H. Bronson. The award recognizes women who have made outstanding contributions to Florida agriculture.

She was also inducted into the Florida Cracker Hall of Fame in 2006 and nominated for the National Cowgirl Hall of Fame in Fort Worth, Texas.

"I love this life," Iris says. "I love the woods and I love working with cattle. I love the honesty and sincerity of it. You can depend on a cowboy when you are in the woods. A cowboy will always help you. Once you're a cowhunter, you're always a cowhunter."